A Woman's Journey

Reflections on Life, Love, and Happiness

A Woman's Journey

Reflections on Life, Love, and Happiness

ARIEL BOOKS

ANDREWS *and* McMEEL
KANSAS CITY

ISBN: 0-8362-0742-4

First Printing, July 1995
Third Printing, March 1997

Library of Congress Catalog Card Number: 95-76435

Contents

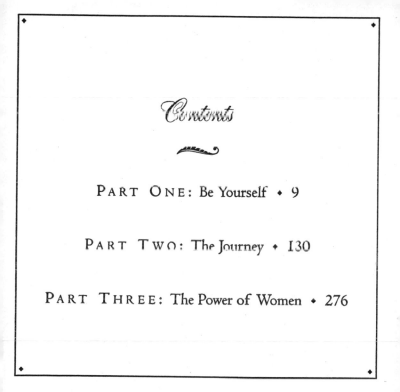

Introduction

*"Our way is not soft grass, it's a mountain path with lots of rocks.
But it goes upwards, forward, toward the sun."*
—DR. RUTH WESTHEIMER

A woman's journey is a difficult one. Often, just when
we think the road smoothes out, we come to a fork, a sharp
curve, or a steep hill. Equipped with determination, courage,
and a sense of humor, we stumble up some hills and breeze

over others. Either way, we experience personal satisfaction and gain confidence.

In a world where we are urged to change to fit the current fashion, it takes courage to be ourselves. Years ago women with a pioneering spirit crossed into male-dominated fields and proceeded to excel in the worlds of science, sports, politics, and finance. But whether we're riding the A-train to Wall Street, or wallpapering the baby's bedroom, we're choosing where and what we want to be.

This inspirational book will be a great companion on your personal trek. Women from various backgrounds and fields speak of the importance of finding out who we are and of the personal power that comes with that discovery. A woman's journey is a challenging one, but it's the only road that will take her home—to herself.

PART ONE: *Be Yourself*

*W*hy not be oneself? That is the whole secret of a successful appearance. If one is a greyhound why try to look like a Pekinese?

Edith Sitwell

*We have to dare
to be ourselves, however
frightening or strange that self
may prove to be.*

— **MAY SARTON**

I too am a rare
Pattern. As I wander down
The garden paths.

AMY LOWELL

Love yourself first and
everything else falls into line.
You really have to love yourself to get
anything done in this world.

— *Lucille Ball*

*What I wanted to be
when I grew up was
— in charge.*

WILMA VAUGHT

$\mathscr{F}$riendship with oneself is all
important, because without it
one cannot be friends with anyone else
in the world.

~ *Eleanor Roosevelt* ~

Trust your gut.

BARBARA WALTERS

When I stand before God at the end of my life, I would hope that I would not have a single bit of talent left and could say, "I used everything you gave me."

Erma Bombeck

I long to accomplish a great and noble task, but it is my chief duty to accomplish small tasks as if they were great and noble.

~ Helen Keller ~

It is never too late to be what you might have been.

GEORGE ELIOT

That's the risk you take
if you change: that people you've been
involved with won't like the new you.
But other people who do
will come along.

Lisa Alther

*I*t is ridiculous to take on a man's job just in order to be able to say that 'a woman has done it—yah!' The only decent reason for tackling a job is that it is *your* job, and *you* want to do it.

— Dorothy Sayers —

Worry less about what other people think about you, and more about what you think of them.

FAY WELDON

If you do not tell the truth about yourself you cannot tell it about other people.

Virginia Woolf

One of the sad commentaries
on the way women are viewed
in our society is that we have to
fit one category. I have never felt
that I had to be in one category.

Faye Wattleton

I wouldn't give you a dime
for my seat in the Senate
if I couldn't vote according
to my convictions and conscience.

Hattie W. Caraway

*It is not easy to be sure
that being yourself is worth the
trouble, but [we do know]
it is our sacred duty.*

FLORIDA SCOTT-MAXWELL

I am a woman who enjoys herself very much; sometimes I lose, sometimes I win.

MATA HARI

I was thought to be "stuck up." I wasn't. I was just sure of myself. This is and always has been an unforgivable quality to the unsure.

— *Bette Davis* —

I looked on child rearing not only as a work of love and duty but as a profession that was fully as interesting and challenging as any honorable profession in the world and one that demanded the best that I could bring to it.

Rose Kennedy

I am only one; but still I am one.

I cannot do everything,

but still I can do something.

I will not refuse to do the

something I can do.

~ Helen Keller ~

Just as you inherit your mother's brown eyes, you inherit part of yourself.

ALICE WALKER

Whatever you want in life, other people are going to want, too. Believe in yourself enough to accept the idea that *you have an equal right to it.*

— Diane Sawyer —

I own my life. And only mine.
And so I shall appreciate my person.
And so I shall make proper
use of myself.

— *Ruth Beebe Hill* —

*Just don't give up trying to
do what you really want to do.
Where there is love and inspiration,
I don't think you can go wrong.*

— Ella Fitzgerald —

I know what it means to be a miner and a cowboy, and have risked my life when need be, *but*, best of all, I have felt the charm of the glorious freedom, the quick rushing blood, the bounding motion, of the wild life, the joy of the living and of the doing, of the mountain and the plain; I have learned to know and feel some, at least, of the secrets of the Wild Ones.

Grace Seton-Thompson

Women . . . often . . . need to return
to their past, to the women who were
part of that past, to girlhood when a self existed
that was individual and singular,
defined neither by men, nor children, nor home,
almost as though with layers of roles and
responsibilities they have covered over a real person
and must now peel back those layers and reclaim
the self that was just emerging in adolescence.

Mary Helen Washington

*We are the hero
of our own story.*

MARY MCCARTHY

I still want to do my work, I still want to do my livingness. And I have lived. I have been fulfilled. I recognized what I had, and I never sold it short. And I ain't through yet!

~ *Louise Nevelson* ~

Think wrongly,
if you please, but in all cases
think for yourself.

DORIS LESSING

In my early days I was a sepia Hedy Lamarr. Now I'm black and a woman, singing my own way.

LENA HORNE

There is nothing Madison Avenue
can give us that will make us
more beautiful women.
We are beautiful
because God created us that way.

Marianne Williamson

*You can be pleased
with nothing when you are
not pleased with yourself.*

———

**LADY
MARY WORTLEY MONTAGU**

Long tresses down to the floor can be beautiful, if you have that, but learn to love what you have.

ANITA BAKER

A life of reaction is a life of slavery, intellectually and spiritually. One must fight for a life of action, not reaction.

RITA MAE BROWN

*Don't try to be such
a perfect girl, darling.
Do the best you can without
too much anxiety or strain.*

Jesse Barnard

*F*ate cast me to play the role of an ugly duckling with no promise of swanning. Therefore, I sat down when a mere child—fully realizing just how *utterly* "mere" I was—and figured out my life early. Most people do it, but they do it too late. At any rate, from the beginning I have played my life as a comedy rather than the tragedy many would have made of it.

Marie Dressler

*L*et the world know you
as you are, not as you think
you should be, because sooner or later,
if you are posing, you will forget the
pose, and then where are you?

Fanny Brice

I have fought and kicked and fasted and prayed and cursed and cried myself to the point of existing. It has been like being born again, literally. Just *knowing* has meant everything to me. Knowing has pushed me out into the world, into college, into places, into people.

Alice Walker

I was raised to sense
what someone wanted me to be
and be that kind of person.
It took me a long time not to judge
myself through someone else's eyes.

Sally Field

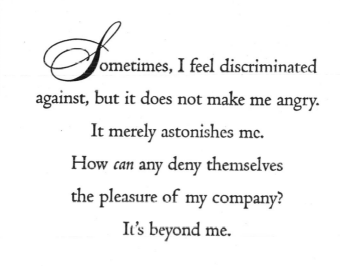

*S*ometimes, I feel discriminated against, but it does not make me angry. It merely astonishes me. How *can* any deny themselves the pleasure of my company? It's beyond me.

— *Zora Neale Hurston*

I argue that we deserve the choice to do whatever we want with our faces and bodies without being punished by an ideology that is using attitudes, economic pressure, and even legal judgments regarding women's appearance to undermine us psychologically and politically.

Naomi Wolf

I had found a kind of serenity, a new maturity. . . . I didn't feel better or stronger than anyone else but it seemed no longer important whether everyone loved me or not—more important now was for me to love them. Feeling that way turns your whole life around; living becomes the act of giving. When I do a performance now, I still need and like the adulation of an audience, of course, but my *real* satisfaction comes from what I have given of myself, from the joyful act of singing itself.

Beverly Sills

*You've got to take the
initiative and play your game
. . . . confidence makes
the difference.*

CHRIS EVERT

Learning to live with
what you're born with
is the process,
the involvement,
the making of a life.

DIANE WAKOSKI

I'd gone through life believing
in the strength and competence of
others; never in my own. Now, dazzled,
I discovered that *my* capacities were real.
It was like finding a fortune in
the lining of an old coat.

Joan Mills

*How many cares one loses
when one decides not to be
something, but to be someone.*

Coco Chanel

Maybe the less pain
women inflict on their bodies,
the more beautiful
our bodies will look to us.

NAOMI WOLF

A liberated woman is
one who feels confident in herself, and is
happy in what she is doing.
She is a person who has a sense of
self . . . It all comes down to
freedom of choice.

Betty Ford

*I never painted dreams.
I painted my own reality.*

~

FRIDA KAHLO

To do good things in the world, first you must know who you are and what gives meaning in your life.

PAULA P. BROWNLEE

While I can't say there was a
particular moment when I attended a
concert, heard a piece and was
overwhelmed, music was always around,
and I just sang for the pleasure of it.

Barbara Hendricks

*Y*ou must not think that I feel,
in spite of it having ended in such
defeat, that my "life has been wasted"
here, or that I would exchange it
with that of anyone I know.

Isak Dinesen

Women are not inherently passive or peaceful. We're not inherently anything but human.

ROBIN MORGAN

I see no reason to keep silent about my enjoyment of the sound of my own voice as I work.

MURIEL SPARK

I am not eccentric. It's just that *I* am more alive than most people. *I* am an unpopular electric eel set in a pond of goldfish.

EDITH SITWELL

*S*he had nothing to fall back on;
not maleness, not whiteness,
not ladyhood, not anything. And out of
the profound desolation of her reality
she may well have invented herself.

Toni Morrison

*Believing in our hearts
that who we are is enough
is the key to a more satisfying
and balanced life.*

ELLEN SUE STERN

*Inside myself is a place
where I live alone and that's
where you renew your springs
that never dry up.*

PEARL S. BUCK

*I rarely draw
what I see.
I draw what I feel
in my body.*

Barbara Hepworth

When you're young and someone tells you what you are and shows you how to be proud, you've got a head start.

VIKKI CARR

*I've never had a day when
I didn't want to work . . .
In my studio I'm as
happy as a cow in her stall.*

LOUISE NEVELSON

We must overcome the notion that we must be regular . . . it robs you of the chance to be extraordinary and leads you to the mediocre.

UTA HAGEN

Character — the willingness to accept responsibility for one's own life — is the source from which self-respect springs.

JOAN DIDION

It is not easy to find happiness in ourselves, and impossible to find it elsewhere.

AGNES REPPLIER

I seldom think about my limitations, and they never make me sad. Perhaps there is just a touch of yearning at times; but it is vague, like a breeze among flowers.

Helen Keller

*We don't know
who we are until
we see what we can do.*

MARTHA GRIMES

*The best compliment they [men]
can give a woman is that she thinks
like a man. I say she does not;
she thinks like a woman.*

Margaret Thatcher

It's hard to stay committed . . . to stay in touch with the goal without saying there's something wrong with myself, my goal, the world.

~ *Nancy Hogshead* ~

You have to have confidence in your ability, and then be tough enough to follow through.

ROSALYNN CARTER

*I*t's this no-nonsense side of
women that is pleasant to deal with.
They are the real sportsmen.
They don't have to be constantly building
up frail egos by large public performances
like over-tipping the hat-check girl,
speaking fluent French to
the Hungarian waiter, and sending
back the wine to be recooled.

Phyllis McGinley

I really do believe I can accomplish a great deal with a big grin. I know some people find that disconcerting, but that doesn't matter.

~ Beverly Sills ~

I never intended to become a run-of-the-mill person.

BARBARA JORDAN

A woman who is willing to be herself and pursue her own potential runs not so much the risk of loneliness as the challenge of exposure to more interesting men—and people in general.

Lorraine Hansberry

I had already learned from more than a decade of political life that I was going to be criticized no matter what I did, so I might as well be criticized for something I wanted to do. (If I had spent all day 'pouring tea,' I would have been criticized for that too.)

Rosalynn Carter

*One can never consent
to creep when one feels
an impulse to soar.*

HELEN KELLER

What really matters
is what you do with
what you have.

SHIRLEY LORD

A woman who has no way of expressing herself and of realizing herself as a human being has nothing else to turn to but the owning of material things.

Enriqueta Longauex y Vasquez

*Who I am
is the best I can be.*

—

LEONTYNE PRICE

The more independent you want to be, the more generous you must be with yourself as a woman.

DIANE VON FURSTENBERG

You need only claim the events of your life to make yourself yours. When you truly possess all you have been and done, which may take some time, you are fierce with reality.

Florida
Scott-Maxwell

I have a right to my anger,
and I don't want anybody telling me
I shouldn't be, that it's not nice to be,
and that something's wrong with me
because I get angry.

~ *Maxine Waters* ~

I feel that what we must say to
one another is based on encouraging
each of us to be true to herself:
"Now that we are equal,
let us dare to be *different!* "

~ *Maria de Lourdes*
Pintasilgo

There are people who put their
dreams in a little box and say,
"Yes, I've got dreams, of course, I've got dreams."
Then they put the box away and
bring it out once in awhile to look in it,
and yep, they're still there. These are *great* dreams,
but they never even get out of the box.
It takes an uncommon amount of guts to put your
dreams on the line, to hold them up and say,
"How good or how bad am I?"
That's where courage comes in.

Erma Bombeck

*I'll walk where my own
nature would be leading —
It vexes me to choose
another guide.*

EMILY BRONTË

*T*he fact is, I can have any experience of life I want. I don't have to choose any one thing or act in any one way to define myself as a woman now. I am one.

Ally Sheedy

*I've always been
independent, and I don't
see how it conflicts
with femininity.*

SYLVIA PORTER

Until you make peace with who you are, you'll never be content with what you have.

DORIS MORTMAN

*U*nless I am what I am
and feel what I feel—as hard as I can
and as honestly and truly as I can—
then I am nothing. Let me feel
guilt . . . don't try to educate
me . . . don't protect me.

Elizabeth Janeway

I am still learning—how to take joy in all the people I am, how to use all my selves in the service of what I believe, how to accept when I fail and rejoice when I succeed.

Audre Lorde

Every time you don't follow your inner guidance, you feel a loss of energy, loss of power, a sense of spiritual deadness.

SHAKTI GAWAIN

*F*or a long time the only time
I felt beautiful—in the sense of being
complete as a woman, as a human
being—was when I was singing.

Leontyne Price

It was on that road and at that hour that I first became aware of my own self, experienced an inexpressible state of grace, and felt one with the first breath of air that stirred, the first bird, and the sun so newly born that it still looked not quite round.

Colette

I am what I am.
Take it or leave me alone.

~~~

ROSARIO MORALES

I am playing with my Self,

I am playing with the world's soul,

I am the dialogue between my Self and

el espíritu del mundo.

I change myself, I change the world.

— *Gloria Anzaldúa*

We learn best to listen to our own voices if we are listening at the same time to other women . . . whose stories, for all our differences, turn out, if we listen well, to be our stories also.

Barbara Deming

If I didn't define myself
for myself, I would be
crunched into other people's
fantasies for me
and eaten alive.

~

AUDRE LORDE

*There is something
all life has in common,
and when I know what it is
I shall know myself.*

JEAN CRAIGHEAD GEORGE

I cannot and will not cut my conscience to fit this year's fashions.

LILLIAN HELLMAN

You curl your hair and
paint your face.
Not I:
I am curled by the wind,
painted by the sun.

JULIA DE BURGOS

*B*eing solitary is being alone well:
being alone luxuriously immersed in
doings of your own choice, aware of the
fullness of your own presence rather
than of the absence of others.
Because solitude is an achievement.

Alice Koller

Above all, remember that the most important thing you can take anywhere is not a Gucci bag or French-cut jeans; it's an open mind.

GAIL RUBIN BERENY

*Your thorns are
the best part of you.*

~

MARIANNE MOORE

I have no regrets.
I wouldn't have lived my life
the way I did if I was
going to worry about what
people were going to say.

—

INGRID BERGMAN

I will never abdicate. I shall always want everything. To accept my life I must prefer it.

MARIE LENÉRU

*I'm not going to limit
myself just because people won't
accept the fact that
I can do something else.*

DOLLY PARTON

*O*ne day I found myself saying to
myself, "I can't live where I want to.
I can't even say what I want to!
I decided I was a very stupid fool
not to at least paint as I wanted to."

 Georgia O'Keeffe

I am one of those people who just can't help getting a kick out of life — even when it's a kick in the teeth.

POLLY ADLER

*The delights of
self discovery are always
available.*

— GAIL SHEEHY

*L*ong ago I understood that it wasn't merely my being a woman that was preventing my being welcomed into the world of what I long thought of as my peers. It was that I had succeeded in an undertaking few men have even attempted: *I have become myself.*

Alice Koller

I felt so young,
so strong,
so sure of God.

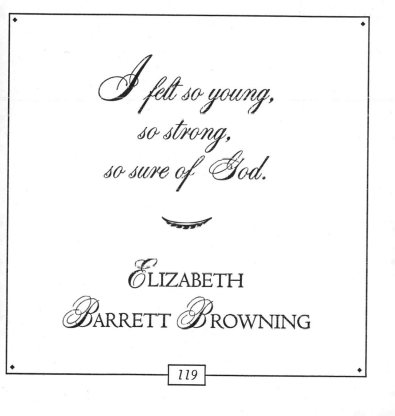

ELIZABETH
BARRETT BROWNING

She would not exchange her solitude for anything. Never again to be forced to move to the rhythms of others.

TILLIE OLSEN

*Let me listen to me
and not to them.*

GERTRUDE STEIN

A woman wins by giving herself and other women permission—to eat; to be sexual; to age; to wear overalls, a paste tiara, a Balenciaga gown, a second-hand opera cloak, or combat boots; to cover up or to go practically naked; *to do whatever we choose* in following—or ignoring —our own aesthetic.

Naomi Wolf

*I've just been so interested
in what I was doing
[genetic research] that I
never thought of stopping.*

❧

BARBARA McCLINTOCK

*The future belongs to those
who believe in the beauty
of their dreams.*

ELEANOR ROOSEVELT

If you haven't forgiven yourself something, how can you forgive others?

DOLORES HUERTA

*I am not afraid to trust
my sisters — not I.*

ANGELINA GRIMKÉ

*We've been taught to
respect our fears, but we must
learn to respect ourselves
and our needs.*

AUDRE LORDE

*W*omen are always being tested . . . but ultimately, each of us has to define who we are individually and then do the very best job we can to grow into that.

Hillary Rodham Clinton

Ultimately,
love is self-approval.

SONDRA RAY

PART TWO: *The Journey*

I soon realized that no journey carries one far unless, as it extends into the world around us, it goes an equal distance into the world within.

Lillian Smith

*Life loves to be taken
by the lapel and be told:
"I am with you kid.
Let's go."*

MAYA ANGELOU

I do not ask to walk smooth paths
nor bear an easy load.
I pray for strength and fortitude
to climb the rock strewn road.
Give me such courage and I can scale
the hardest peaks alone,
And transform every stumbling block
into a stepping stone.

Gail Brook Burket

*I might have been born
in a hovel, but I determined
to travel with the wind
and the stars.*

— JACQUELINE COCHRAN

It's not what you do once in a while, it's what you do day in and day out that makes the difference.

JENNY CRAIG

I had reasoned this out in my mind, there was two things I had a right to, liberty and death. If I could not have one, I would have the other, for no man should take me alive.

— *Harriet Tubman* —

*C*ompetition is easier to accept if you realize it is not an act of oppression or abrasion. . . . I've worked with my best friends in direct competition.

— *Diane Sawyer* —

*Do not wait for leaders;
do it alone, person to person.*

~

MOTHER TERESA

I always wanted to be somebody. If I made it, it's half because I was game enough to take a lot of punishment along the way and half because there were a lot of people who cared enough to help me.

 Althea Gibson

. . . . what matters most is that we learn from living.

DORIS LESSING

*Y*ou must accept that you might fail;

then, if you do your best and still don't win,

at least you can be satisfied that you've tried.

If you don't accept failure as a possibility,

you don't set high goals, you don't branch out,

you don't try—you don't take the risk.

Rosalynn Carter

There are two ways of meeting difficulties: you alter the difficulties or you alter yourself to meet them.

PHYLLIS BOTTOME

Expect nothing.
Live frugally
On surprise.

A LICE W ALKER

I learned . . . that inspiration does not come like a bolt, nor is it kinetic, energetic striving, but it comes into us slowly and quietly and all the time, though we must regularly and every day give it a little chance to start flowing, prime it with a little solitude and idleness.

Brenda Ueland

$\mathcal{M}$y Mother is everywhere . . .
In the perfume of a rose,
The eyes of a tiger,
The pages of a book,
The food that we partake,
The whistling wind of the desert,
The blazing gems of sunset,
The crystal light of full moon,
The opal veils of sunrise.

Grace Seton-Thompson

Make it a rule of life never to regret and never look back. We all live in suspense, from day to day, from hour to hour; in other words, we are the hero of our own story.

— Mary McCarthy

To think too long about doing a thing often becomes its undoing.

EVA YOUNG

I've always believed that one woman's success can only help another woman's success.

GLORIA VANDERBILT

*N*o pessimist ever discovered

the secrets of the stars,

or sailed to an uncharted land,

or opened a new heaven

to the human spirit.

~ *Helen Keller* ~

*A pint can't hold
a quart — if it holds a pint
it is doing all that can
be expected of it.*

MARGARETTA W. DELAND

We write our own destiny.
We become what we do.

MADAME
CHIANG KAI-SHEK

*M*y mother, religious-negro,

proud of having waded through a storm,

is very obviously,

a sturdy Black bridge that I

crossed over, on.

— *Carolyn M. Rodgers*

*I have always had
a dread of becoming
a passenger in life.*

❦

QUEEN MARGRETH II
OF DENMARK

A person can run for years
but sooner or later he has to
take a stand in the place which, for
better or worse, he calls home, do what
he can to change things there.

Paule Marshall

. . . I was taught that the way of progress is neither swift nor easy. . . .

MADAME CURIE

One can never pay in
gratitude; one can only
pay 'in kind' somewhere
else in life.

ANNE MORROW LINDBERGH

*I don't believe in failure.
It is not failure if you
enjoyed the process.*

~

OPRAH WINFREY

*If you really want
something you can figure out
how to make it happen.*

CHER

*P*lease know that I am aware of the hazards. *I want to do it* because I want to do it. Women must try to do things as men have tried. When they fail, their failure must be but a challenge to others.

Amelia Earhart

*Life is either always a
tight-rope or a feather bed.
Give me the tight-rope.*

EDITH WHARTON

When you know to laugh
and when to look upon things
as too absurd to take seriously,
the other person is ashamed to carry
through even if he was serious about it.

Eleanor Roosevelt

My favorite thing is to go where I've never been.

DIANE ARBUS

Too many wish to be happy before becoming wise.

SUSANNE CURCHOD NECKER

Age puzzles me. I thought it
was a quiet time. My seventies were
interesting and fairly serene,
but my eighties are passionate.
I grow more intense as I age.

*Florida
Scott-Maxwell*

Woman softens her own troubles by generously solacing those of others.

―

FRANÇOISE D'AUBEGNE MAINTENON

. . . some of us just go along . . .
until that marvelous day people stop
intimidating us—or should I say we
refuse to let them intimidate us?

Peggy Lee

We are in for a very, very long haul . . .
You will lose your youth, your sleep, your patience,
your sense of humor and occasionally,
the understanding and support of people
who love you very much. In return,
I have nothing to offer you but your pride
in being a woman, and all your dreams
you've ever had for your daughters
and nieces and granddaughters . . .

Jill Ruckelshaus

*M*ama exhorted her children at every opportunity to "jump at de sun." We might not land on the sun, but at least we would get off the ground.

Zora Neale Hurston

Everybody knows if you are too careful you are so occupied in being careful that you are sure to stumble over something.

GERTRUDE STEIN

You grow up the day you have your first real laugh, at yourself.

ETHEL BARRYMORE

*If I had to live my life
again, I'd make the same
mistakes, only sooner.*

TALLULAH BANKHEAD

*O*nce I decide to do something,
I can't have people telling me I can't.
If there's a roadblock, you jump over it,
walk around it, crawl under it.

— Kitty Kelley —

I used to want the words "She tried" on my tombstone. Now I want "She did it."

KATHERINE DUNHAM

The distance is nothing;
it's only the first step
that is difficult.

MARQUISE DU DEFFAND

People create their own questions
because they're afraid to look straight.
All you have to do is look straight and
see the road, and when you see it,
don't sit looking at it—walk.

Ayn Rand

*The need for change
bulldozed a road down
the center of my mind.*

MAYA ANGELOU

I began to have an idea of my life,
not as the slow shaping of achievement
to fit my preconceived purposes,
but as the gradual discovery and growth
of a purpose which I did not know.

Joanna Field

*No life is so hard
that you can't make it easier
by the way you take it.*

ELLEN GLASGOW

Far away there in the sunshine are
my highest aspirations. I may not reach
them but I can look up and see
their beauty, believe in them and
try to follow them.

Louisa May Alcott

I think these difficult times have helped me to understand better than before how *infinitely* rich and beautiful life is in every way and that so many things that one goes around worrying about are of no importance whatsoever.

~ *Isak Dinesen* ~

*I*n the first grade, I already knew the pattern of my life. I didn't know the living of it, but I knew the line. . . . From the first day in school until the day I graduated, everyone gave me one hundred plus in art. Well, where do you go in life? You go to the place where you got one hundred plus.

Louise Nevelson

*I*nquisitiveness and strength make me want to rise above my valley-bound brothers. I must reach the summit to see the truth.

— *Delores Seats* —

*W*hatever you do, don't give up. Because all you can do once you've given up is bitch. I've known some great bitchers in my time. With some it's a passion, with others an art.

— *Molly Ivins* —

*I want to be all that I
am capable of becoming. . . .*

KATHERINE MANSFIELD

It's very important to define
success for *yourself*. If you really
want to reach for the brass ring,
just remember that there are
sacrifices that go along.

~ *Cathleen Black* ~

Doing the best at this moment puts you in the best place for the next moment.

OPRAH WINFREY

Courageous risks are life giving, they help you grow, make you brave and better than you think you are.

JOAN L. CURCIO

I look back on my life like a good day's work, it was done and I am satisfied with it.

GRANDMA MOSES

I've never sought success in order to get fame and money; it's the talent and the passion that count in success.

INGRID BERGMAN

If we don't change,
we don't grow.
If we don't grow,
we are not really living.

GAIL SHEEHY

I live a day at a time.
Each day I look for a kernel of
excitement. In the morning, I say:
"What is my exciting thing for today?"
Then, I do the day.
Don't ask me about tomorrow.

Barbara Jordan

Do not follow where the path may lead. Go instead where there is no path and leave a trail.

MURIEL STRODE

How wrong it is for woman to expect the man to build the world she wants, rather than set out to create it herself.

ANAÏS NIN

I have always grown from my problems and challenges, from the things that don't work out, that's when I've really learned.

CAROL BURNETT

It is no sin to attempt and fail. The only sin is not to make the attempt.

SUELLEN FRIED

I long to put the experience of fifty years at once into your young lives, to give you at once the key to that treasure chamber every gem of which has cost me tears and struggles and prayers, but you must work for these inward treasures yourselves.

Harriet Beecher Stowe

As I grow older, part of my emotional survival plan must be to actively seek inspiration instead of passively waiting for it to find me.

— *Bebe Moore Campbell*

*All serious daring
starts from within.*

EUDORA WELTY

It is necessary to try to pass one's self always; this occupation ought to last as long as life.

QUEEN CHRISTINA
OF SWEDEN

*Like all people
who have nothing,
I lived on dreams.*

ANZIA YEZIERSKA

We don't make mistakes.
We just have learnings.

—

ANNE WILSON SCHAEF

*O*ne only gets to the top rung on
the ladder by steadily climbing up one at
a time, and suddenly all sorts of powers,
all sorts of abilities . . . become within
your own possibility and you think,
'Well, I'll have a go, too.'

Margaret Thatcher

Choose to have a career early and a family late. Or choose to have a family early and a career late — *but plan a long life.*

Dr. Janet Davison Rowley

I've always tried to go a step past wherever people expected me to end up.

BEVERLY SILLS

Life is change.
Growth is optional.
Choose wisely.

KAREN KAISER CLARK

I don't want to get to
the end of my life and find that
I just lived the length of it.
I want to have lived the width
of it as well.

Diane Ackerman

To believe in something
not yet proved and to
underwrite it with our lives;
it is the only way we can
leave the future open.

LILLIAN SMITH

*T*here is no such thing as *can't*, only *won't*.
If you're qualified, all it takes is a burning desire
to accomplish, to make a change.
Go forward, go backward. Whatever it takes!
But you can't blame other people or society
in general. It all comes from your mind.
When we do the impossible
we realize we are special people.

Jan Ashford

I was brought up to believe
that the only thing worth doing
was to add to the sum of accurate
information in the world.

 Margaret Mead

Going into the wilderness
involves the wilderness within us all.
This may be the deepest value of such
an experience, the recognition of our
kinship with the natural world.

~ *China Galland* ~

*Be bold. If you're going
to make an error,
make a doozy, and don't be
afraid to hit the ball.*

BILLIE JEAN KING

I've dreamt in my life dreams that have stayed with me ever after, and changed my ideas: they've gone through and through me, like wine through water, and altered the color of my mind.

Emily Brontë

*For me life is a challenge.
And it will be a challenge if
I live to be 100 or if
I get to be a trillionaire.*

BEAH RICHARDS

When you make a world
tolerable for yourself,
you make a world tolerable
for others.

Anaïs Nin

*My only advice
is to stay aware,
listen carefully, and
yell for help if you need it.*

JUDY BLUME

The next best thing to winning is losing! At least you've been in the race.

NELLIE HERSHEY TULLIS

The most effective way to do it, is to do it.

Toni Cade Bambara

None of us suddenly becomes something overnight. The preparations have been in the making for a lifetime.

GAIL GODWIN

I have not ceased being fearful,

but I have ceased to let fear control me.

I have accepted fear as a part of life

—specifically the fear of change, the fear of

the unknown; and I have gone ahead despite

the pounding in my heart that says: turn back,

turn back, you'll die if you venture too far.

Erica Jong

Life shrinks or expands in proportion to one's courage.

Anaïs Nin

*T*alk about the joys of the unexpected, can they compare with the joys of the expected, of finding everything delightfully and completely what you knew it was going to be?

Elizabeth Bibesco

Begin somewhere;
you cannot build a reputation
on what you intend to do.

Liz Smith

You gain strength, courage and confidence by every experience in which you really stop to look fear in the face. . . . You must do the thing which you think you cannot do.

 *Eleanor Roosevelt*

As for me,
prizes mean nothing.
My prize is my work.

KATHARINE HEPBURN

Follow your image
as far as you can no matter
how useless you think it is.
Push yourself.

NIKKI GIOVANNI

I think it's the end of progress if you stand still and think of what you've done in the past. I keep on.

LESLIE CARON

I am incapable of conceiving
infinity, and yet I do not accept finity.
I want this adventure that is the context
of my life to go on without end.

Simone de Beauvoir

If I had to live my life over again, I'd dare to make more mistakes next time.

NADINE STAIR

Life's challenges are not supposed to paralyze you, they're supposed to help you discover who you are.

BERNICE JOHNSON REAGON

I've always felt that I would
develop into a really fine actress
because I care more about life beyond
the camera than the life in front of it.

— *Shirley MacLaine* —

Everyone has talent.
What is rare is the courage
to follow the talent to
the dark place where it leads.

ERICA JONG

You have to accept whatever comes and the only important thing is that you meet it with the best you have to give.

ELEANOR ROOSEVELT

*I*f one burdens the future with one's worries, it cannot grow organically. I am filled with confidence, not that I shall succeed in worldly things, but that even when things go badly for me I shall still find life good and worth living.

Etty Hillesum

Where I was born, and where
and how I lived is unimportant.
It is what I have done and where I have
been that should be of interest.

Georgia O'Keeffe

*Don't be afraid your life
will end; be afraid that
it will never begin.*

GRACE HANSEN

While others may argue about whether the world ends with a bang or a whimper, I just want to make sure mine doesn't end with a whine.

— *Barbara Gordon*

*I*f you understand something,
you don't forgive it, you are the thing
itself: forgiveness is for
what you *don't* understand.

~ *Doris Lessing* ~

You must learn day by day,
year by year, to broaden your horizon.
The more things you love, the more you
are interested in, the more you enjoy, the
more you are indignant about, the more
you have left when anything happens.

Ethel Barrymore

If you rest, you rust.

— HELEN HAYES

*W*oman must not accept;
she must challenge. She must not be
awed by that which has been
built up around her; she must reverence
that woman in her which
struggles for expression.

~ *Margaret Sanger* ~

*I hear the singing
of the lives of women,
The clear mystery,
the offering and pride.*

MURIEL RUKEYSER

In the years since I began following the
ways of my grandmothers I have come
to value the teachings, stories, and daily
examples of living which they shared with me.
I pity the younger girls of the future
who will miss out on meeting some
of these fine old women.

Beverly Hungry Wolf

When I look at the future, it's so bright it burns my eyes.

OPRAH WINFREY

No star is ever lost

we once have seen,

We always may be what

we might have been.

ADELAIDE A. PROCTOR

When you get into a tight place and everything goes against you, till it seems as though you could not hang on a minute longer, never give up then, for that is just the place and time that the tide will turn.

Harriet
Beecher Stowe

You may be disappointed if you fail, but you are doomed if you don't try.

BEVERLY SILLS

I don't want to be a passenger in my own life.

~~~

DIANE ACKERMAN

If I can stop one heart from breaking,

I shall not live in vain;

If I can ease one life the aching,

Or cool one pain,

Or help one fainting robin

Unto his nest again,

I shall not live in vain.

Emily Dickinson

$\mathcal{M}$y passions were all gathered

together like fingers that made a fist.

Drive is considered aggression today;

I knew it then as purpose.

Bette Davis

I like living. I have sometimes
been wildly, despairingly, acutely
miserable, racked with sorrow, but
through it all I still know quite certainly
that just to *be alive* is a grand thing.

Agatha Christie

*C*hanges are not only possible
and predictable, but to deny them
is to be an accomplice to one's own
unnecessary vegetation.

Gail Sheehy

No one is so eager to gain new experience as he who doesn't know how to make use of the old ones.

MARIE VON
EBNER-ESCHENBACH

Asserting yourself while respecting others is a very good way to win respect yourself.

JANICE LaROUCHE

I wanted a perfect ending. . . .
Now I've learned, the hard way, that some poems
don't rhyme, and some stories don't have a
clear beginning, middle and end.
Life is about not knowing, having to change,
taking the moment and making the best of it,
without knowing what's going to happen next.
Delicious ambiguity.

Gilda Radner

No song or poem will bear
my mother's name. Yet so many of the
stories that I write, that we all write,
are my mother's stories.

Alice Walker

*L*ife is to be lived. If you have to support yourself, you had bloody well better find some way that is going to be interesting. And you don't do that by sitting around wondering about yourself.

Katharine Hepburn

There are for starters, grandeur and silence, pure water and clean air. There is also the gift of distance . . . the chance to stand away from relationships and daily ritual . . . and the gift of energy. Wilderness infuses us with its own special brand of energy. I remember lying by the Snake River in Idaho once and becoming aware I could not sleep . . . nature's forces had me in hand. I was engulfed by a dance of ions and atoms. My body was responding to the pervasive pull of the moon.

Lynn Thomas

Every day's a kick!

— OPRAH WINFREY

Our way is not soft grass,
it's a mountain path with lots
of rocks. But it goes upwards,
forward, toward the sun.

Dr. Ruth Westheimer

*F*inancial success comes second.
My greatest accomplishment is
raising my children to be caring,
contributing members of the world.

Caroline
 Rose Hunt

*L*et me stand in my age with
all its waters flowing round me.
If they sometimes subdue, they must
finally upbear me, for I seek the
universal—and that must be the best.

Margaret Fuller

I'm cautious about making money at something that is not the love of my life.

EMILY PRAGER

I could not, at any age, be content to
take my place in a corner by the
fireside and simply look on.
Life was meant to be lived. Curiosity must be
kept alive. The fatal thing is the rejection.
One must never, for whatever reason,
turn his back on life.

Eleanor Roosevelt

The ultimate lesson all of us have to learn is *unconditional love*, which includes not only others but ourselves as well.

Elisabeth Kübler-Ross

If you play it safe in life you've decided that you don't want to grow anymore.

SHIRLEY HUFSTEDLER

I will not be just a tourist in the world of images, just watching images passing by which I cannot live in, make love to, possess as permanent sources of joy and ecstasy.

 *Anaïs Nin*

I don't care about the Oscar.
I make movies to support the causes
I believe in, not for any honors.
I couldn't care less whether
I win an Oscar or not.

Jane Fonda

The only people who never fail are those who never try.

ILKA CHASE

You may have a fresh start
any moment you choose,
for this thing that we call 'failure'
is not the falling down,
but the staying down.

Mary Pickford

I have always been driven by some distant music—a battle hymn no doubt—for I have been at war from the beginning. I've never looked back before. I've never had the time and it has always seemed so dangerous. To look back is to relax one's vigil.

Bette Davis

I love my past.

I love my present.

I'm not ashamed of what I've had,

and I'm not sad because

I have it no longer.

Colette

I am not afraid of storms
for I am learning
to sail my ship.

LOUISA MAY ALCOTT

I postpone death by living,
by suffering, by error,
by risking, by giving,
by losing.

ANAÏS NIN

We older women who know
we aren't heroines can offer
our younger sisters, at the very least,
an honest report of what we have
learned and how we have grown.

Elizabeth Janeway

*O*f course I realized there was a measure of danger. Obviously I faced the possibility of not returning when first I considered going. Once faced and settled there really wasn't any good reason to refer to it.

Amelia Earhart

I do not want to die . . . until
I have faithfully made the most of my
talent and cultivated the seed that
was placed in me until the last
small twig has grown.

Käthe Kollwitz

PART THREE: *The Power of Women*

There does not have to be powerlessness.
The power is within ourselves.

Faye Wattleton

*If [women] understood
and exercised their power
they could remake the world.*

~

EMILY TAFT DOUGLAS

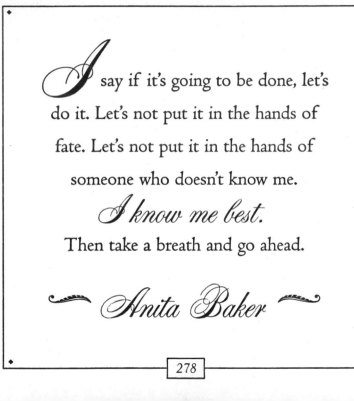

I say if it's going to be done, let's do it. Let's not put it in the hands of fate. Let's not put it in the hands of someone who doesn't know me. *I know me best.* Then take a breath and go ahead.

Anita Baker

The curious fascination in this job
is the illusion that either you are
being useful or you could be—and
that's so tempting.

Millicent Fenwick
U. S. representative

No one can make you feel inferior without your consent.

ELEANOR ROOSEVELT

We must not, in trying to think about how we can make a big difference, ignore the small daily differences we can make which, over time, add up to big differences that we often cannot foresee.

Marian Wright Edelman

*From a timid, shy girl
I had become a woman of
resolute character, who could
no longer be frightened
by the struggle with troubles.*

Anna Dostoevsky

*Women have to
summon up courage
to fulfill dormant dreams.*

Alice Walker

*D*uring the month of June I acted as a pony express rider carrying the U.S. mail between Deadwood and Custer, a distance of fifty miles . . . It was considered the most dangerous route in the Hills, but as my reputation as a rider and quick shot was well known, I was molested very little, for the toll gatherers looked on me as being a good fellow, and they knew that I never missed my mark.

Martha Jane Burke

As a woman, I have no country. . . . As a woman my country is the whole world.

VIRGINIA WOOLF

When people keep telling you that you can't do a thing, you kind of like to try it.

~

MARGARET CHASE SMITH

*M*isfortune sprinkles ashes on the head of the man, but falls like dew on the head of the woman, and brings forth gems of strength of which she herself had no conscious possession.

Anna Cora Mowatt

You have to ask the questions
and attempt to find answers,
because you're right in the middle of it;
they've put you in charge—and
during a hurricane, too.

Sheila Ballantyne

In whatever situation we are placed, our greater or less degree of happiness must be derived from ourselves. Happiness is in a great measure the result of our own dispositions and actions.

Hannah Webster Foster

I try to balance my life.
When I'm home, I give quality time . . .
I'm happy I've achieved what I have
without losing my head.

PATTI LABELLE

*U*nfortunately, there are still many women in the business world who refuse to support women. I call them "Honorary Males"—women who think that power is to be had only in the company of men. Women must realize they have power—economic and political. Don't give your power away; use it for yourself and for the benefit of other women.

Ginger Purdy

*. . . .as one goes through
life one learns that if you
don't paddle your own canoe,
you don't move.*

KATHARINE HEPBURN

*Woman must not depend
upon the protection of man,
but must be taught
to protect herself.*

SUSAN B. ANTHONY

*D*on't shut yourself up in a
bandbox because you are a woman,
but understand what is going on,
and educate yourself to take part in the world's
work for it all affects you and yours.

Louisa May Alcott

LITTLE WOMEN

*A*ll my life I've been competing—and competing to win. I came to realize that in its way, this cancer was the toughest competition I'd faced yet. I made up my mind that I was going to lick it all the way. I not only wasn't going to let it kill me, I wasn't even going to let it put me on the shelf.

Babe Didrikson Zaharias

A woman is like a tea bag. You never know how strong she is until she gets into hot water.

ELEANOR ROOSEVELT

Women's place is in the House — and in the Senate.

GLORIA SCHAFFER

*M*y will shall shape my future. Whether I fail or succeed shall be no man's doing but my own. I am the force; I can clear any obstacle before me or I can be lost in the maze. My choice; my responsibility; win or lose, only I hold the key to my destiny.

Elaine Maxwell

We should try to bring to any power what we have as women. We will destroy it all if we try to imitate that absolutely unfeeling, driving ambition that we have seen coming at us across the desk.

— Colleen Dewhurst —

*A*nd now that I don't want to
own anything any more and am free,
now I suddenly own everything,
now my *inner riches*
are immeasurable.

~ *Etty Hillesum* ~

*T*he Met was the first mountain
I climbed successfully. I had said no to
them when I felt I wasn't ready.
When I debuted, I was technically
prepared and highly negotiable.
I was box-office.

— Leontyne Price —

*I'll stay until
I'm tired of it. So long as
Britain needs me,
I shall never be tired of it.*

MARGARET THATCHER

*N*ow the real beginnings of the
"freedom" which we have discussed for many
years—and a heady freedom it is,
coming after so many years of reaching
outward for it—to finally discover
all I had to do was reach inward,
and it was there waiting all the time for me!

Alisa Wells

*N*o coward soul is mine,

No trembler in the world's

storm-troubled sphere:

I see Heaven's glories shine,

And faith shines equal,

arming me from fear.

— Emily Brontë —

*E*ach story is like a new challenge
or a new adventure and I don't
find help anywhere, or look for it
anywhere, except inside.

 *Eudora Welty*

A women's organization was the catalyst to trigger a flip-flop in my mind that I wasn't a follower, I was a leader. And in spite of my first reaction, that of fear, and a feeling I couldn't do it, I took the risk. Don't listen to other people's negativity; they filter through their own experiences. Learn to trust your own feelings. If you feel in your gut you have a winner, you have to do it no matter what.

Ginger Purdy

*. . . women are
the architects of society.*

HARRIET BEECHER STOWE

We are the curators of
life on earth.
We hold it in the palm
of our hand.

HELEN CALDICOTT

You don't get to choose how
you're going to die.
Or when. You can only decide
how you're going to live.
Now.

Joan Baez

I realized that public affairs
were also *my* affairs. I became active in
politics because I saw the possibility,
if we all sat back and did nothing,
of a world in which there would no longer
be any stages for actors to act on.

Helen Gahagan Douglas

The acceptance of women as authority figures or as role models is an important step in female education. . . . It is this process of identification, respect, and then self-respect that promotes growth.

— Judy Chicago —

I need to take an emotional breath, step back, and remind myself who's actually in charge of my life.

JUDITH M. KNOWLTON

The especial genius of women
I believe to be electrical in
movement, intuitive in
function, spiritual in tendency.

MARGARET FULLER

Life is what we make it,
always has been,
always will be.

~

GRANDMA MOSES

I am never afraid
of what I know.

ANNA SEWELL

To be one woman, truly,
wholly, is to be all women.
Tend one garden and
you will birth worlds.

KATE BRAVERMAN

*It's better to be a lion
for a day than a sheep
all your life.*

SISTER ELIZABETH KENNY

I became more courageous by doing the very things I needed to be courageous for—first, a little, and badly. Then, bit by bit, more and better. Being avidly—sometimes annoyingly—curious and persistent about discovering how others were doing what I wanted to do.

Audre Lorde

The woman who has sprung free has emotional mobility. She is able to move toward the things that are satisfying to her and away from those that are not. She is free, also, to succeed.

Colette Dowling

. . . women are carrying a new attitude.
They've cast aside the old stereotypes.
They don't believe you have to be ugly
or have big muscles to play sports.

 Shirley Johnson

*I*f the first woman God ever made was
strong enough to turn the world upside
down all alone, these women together
ought to be able to turn it back,
and get it right side up again!
And now they is asking to do it,
the men better let them.

Sojourner Truth

*That is what learning is.
You suddenly understand
something you've understood all
your life, but in a new way.*

DORIS LESSING

*O*nce you live with the issue of women
and the landscape for a while,
you find that you cannot separate them from the
notions of peace, spirituality, and community.
As women we must learn to become
leaders in society, not just for our own sake,
but for the sake of all people.
We must support and protect our
kinship with the environment
for the generations to come.

China Galland

$\mathcal{P}$ower is strength and the ability to

see yourself through your own eyes

and not through the eyes of another.

It is being able to place a circle of power

at your own feet and not take power

from someone else's circle.

Lynn V. Andrews

But the whole point of liberation is that you get out. Restructure your life. Act by yourself.

JANE FONDA

*I have a lot of things
to prove to myself.
One is that I can live
my life fearlessly.*

~

OPRAH WINFREY

Women need to see ourselves as individuals capable of creating change. That is what political and economic power is all about: *having a voice, being able to shape the future.* Women's absence from decision-making positions has deprived the country of a necessary perspective.

Madeleine Kunin

I've always wanted to equalize things for us . . . Women can be great athletes. And I think we'll find in the next decade that women athletes will finally get the attention they deserve.

Billie Jean King

All things are possible until they are proved impossible — even the impossible may only be so, as of now.

PEARL S. BUCK

The two important things I did learn were that you are as powerful and strong as you allow yourself to be, and that the most difficult part of any endeavor is taking the first step, making the first decision.

Robyn Davidson

I am old enough to know that victory is often a thing deferred, and rarely at the summit of courage . . . What is at the summit of courage, I think, is freedom. The freedom that comes with the knowledge that no earthly thing can break you.

Paula Giddings

The challenges of change are always hard.
It is important that we begin to unpack those
challenges that confront this nation and
realize that we each have a role that
requires *us* to change and become more
responsible for shaping our own future.

Hillary Rodham Clinton

Our strength is often composed of the weaknesses we're damned if we're going to show.

MIGNON McLAUGHLIN

*T*here *is* a fountain of youth:

it is your mind, your talents,

the creativity you bring to your life and

the lives of people you love.

When you learn to tap this source,

you will truly have defeated age.

— *Sophia Loren* —

May you have the strength to enjoy your weaknesses.

FLORENCE EDWARDS

I am not belittling the brave
pioneer men, but the sunbonnet as well
as the sombrero has helped to settle
this glorious land of ours.

Edna Ferber

*Fear grows in darkness;
if you think there's a
bogeyman around,
turn on the light.*

DOROTHY THOMPSON

To be a leader you must feel that you are both everything and nothing —nothing in that you are on this earth for a few years out of billions . . . everything, because you are at the center of all activity in your world.

Edith Weiner

I believe in my work and the joy of it. You have to be with the work and the work has to be with you. It absorbs you totally and you absorb it totally. Everything must fall by the wayside by comparison.

— *Louise Nevelson* —

*Never grow a wishbone,
daughter, where your
backbone ought to be.*

— CLEMENTINE PADDLEFORD

When self-respect takes it
rightful place in the psyche
of woman, she will not allow herself
to be manipulated by anyone.

Indira Mahindra

. . . I can do what I want to do and that has been my greatest gift.

FAITH RINGGOLD

*I don't know everything,
I just do everything.*

———

TONI MORRISON

I discovered I always have choices and sometimes it's only a choice of attitude.

JUDITH M. KNOWLTON

*I*f you don't like the way
the world is, you change it.
You have an obligation to change it.
You just do it one step at a time.

Marian
Wright Edelman

There's some kind of courage and independence in a woman who's had to work hard all her life.

DONNA REDMOND

I see something that has to be done and I organize it.

ELINOR GUGGENHEIMER

I have a brain and a uterus, and I use both.

PATRICIA SCHROEDER

*I*t is for us to pray not for tasks
equal to our powers, but for powers
equal to our tasks, to go forward
with a great desire forever beating
at the door of our hearts as we
travel towards our distant goal.

Helen Keller

*I*t's lucky happenstance that women's liberation came along just when it did so that women can participate in the world arena and rescue the planet. Just in the nick of time.

Gretchen Cryer

There is a growing strength in women, but it's in the forehead, not in the forearm.

BEVERLY SILLS

*. . . I'm not going
to lie down and let
trouble walk over me.*

ELLEN GLASGOW

Women share with men the need for personal success, even the taste for power, and no longer are we willing to satisfy those needs through the achievements of surrogates, whether husbands, children or merely role models.

 Elizabeth Dole

You really can change the world if you care enough.

~

MARIAN WRIGHT EDELMAN

Don't be afraid of the space between your dreams and reality. If you can dream it, you can make it so.

BELVA DAVIS

*Suddenly many movements
are going on within me,
many things are happening, there is an
almost unbearable sense of sprouting,
of bursting encasements,
of moving kernels, expanding flesh.*

— Meridel Le Sueur

*If you think you can,
you can. And if you think
you can't, you're right.*

―

MARY KAY ASH

I realized that if what we
call human nature can be changed,
then absolutely anything is possible.
And from that moment,
my life changed.

Shirley MacLaine

It's better to have a rich soul than to be rich.

OLGA KORBUT

A strong woman artist who is not afraid of herself, her sexuality, passion, symbols, language, who is fearless, willing to take any and all risks, often produces work that is staggeringly beautiful and at the same time frightening, dangerous, something to be reckoned with.

Laura Farabough

*She knew what all
smart women knew:
Laughter made you
live better and longer.*

GAIL PARENT

*H*umor is such a strong weapon,
such a strong answer. Women have
to make jokes about themselves,
laugh about themselves,
because they have nothing to lose.

~ *Agnes Varda* ~

*I knew someone had
to take the first step and
I made up my mind
not to move.*

ROSA PARKS

I don't think there's anything in the world I can't do . . . In my creative source, whatever that is, I don't see why I can't sculpt. Why shouldn't I? Human beings sculpt. I'm a human being.

 Maya Angelou

When a woman tells the truth she is creating the possibility for more truth around her.

ADRIENNE RICH

Liberation means that I am
confident enough of myself that I can
give it to others, and love means
that I am confident enough
about that other that
I can trust him with my gift.

Carol Travis

I change myself,
I change the world.

GLORIA ANZALDÚA

*S*uccess is often achieved by those who don't know that failure is inevitable.

 Coco Chanel

Don't compromise yourself.

You are all you've got.

JANIS JOPLIN

*N*o matter what happens, keep on beginning and failing. Each time you fail, start all over again, and you will grow stronger until you find that you have accomplished a purpose—not the one you began with perhaps, but one you will be glad to remember.

Anne Sullivan

Life's under no obligation to give us what we expect.

MARGARET MITCHELL

*O*ne is not born a woman,

one becomes one.

~ *Simone de Beauvoir* ~

The great thing about getting older is that you don't lose all the other ages you've been.

MADELINE L'ENGLE

The text of this book was set in Centaur and Swanson

by Harry Chester Inc.

Cover and interior design

by Judith Stagnitto Abbate